GARBAGE
HELPS OUR GARDEN GROW

A Compost Story

STORY BY **Linda Glaser**   PHOTOGRAPHY BY **Shelley Rotner**

M MILLBROOK PRESS / MINNEAPOLIS

At our house, we grow lettuce and tomatoes, pumpkins and potatoes, strawberries, sunflowers, cucumbers, and cauliflowers.

And we use garbage to do it!

This is where it starts—in our compost bin.
It's just a big box. But amazing things happen here.

First, we collect the garbage—cantaloupe rinds and Dad's coffee grounds from breakfast, leftover lettuce from lunch, old broccoli from the fridge, and peanut shells from our snack.

Here it goes! We toss it all in.

Here's a moldy jack-o'-lantern that we carved for Halloween.
It doesn't look like much anymore. But it's still good for something.
It's good for the compost. So we dump it in.

All fall and winter, our pumpkins will stay here—just rotting away.

We also toss in grass clippings and fallen leaves from our yard, old chopped-up cucumber vines from the garden, and all our wilted flowers— daisies, dahlias, sweet peas, and sunflowers.

Layer after layer. Leftovers from our plates and leftovers from our garden all end up in our compost bin.

Sometimes I spray the pile with water to keep it nice and moist.

Sometimes our friends come and help in the garden. We all watch when Mom takes her pitchfork and tosses the whole pile.

Worms help in our compost bin too!
They eat the rotting food and leaves. And
slowly, slowly the food and leaves change.

Sometimes you can feel heat coming from the compost.
If you dig down deep, you can sometimes even see steam.

That's when you know the garbage is changing. It's called decay. That's nature's way of recycling.

Amazing! The compost doesn't even smell like garbage. It smells fresh like earth. And it doesn't look like garbage. It looks like dark brown soil.

Now it's ready to go into our garden. We fill our shovels and spread the compost all around.

Then we mix and dig,
mix and dig.

Now we plant lettuce and tomatoes, pumpkins and potatoes, strawberries, sunflowers, cucumbers, and cauliflowers.

Look what sprouted in our compost bin—pumpkin seeds from
our old jack-o'-lantern! We take the little seedlings and plant them too.

By fall, they'll grow into long green vines
with big orange pumpkins.

Compost makes the earth rich. It helps our
garden grow and grow . . . and grow!

The more we compost, the less garbage we throw out.
And less garbage ends up in the landfill.
Composting is good for the earth—in more ways than one!

So that's how composting works. It keeps on going around and around from garbage to compost to garden again and again and again.

QUESTIONS AND ANSWERS ABOUT COMPOSTING

For adults who might want to start composting with children, here are the answers to some questions you might have.

WHAT'S THE EASIEST WAY TO MAKE COMPOST?

Pile dry fallen leaves and grass clippings in a corner of your backyard. Layer it—leaves and grass, leaves and grass, leaves and grass, using more leaves than grass. Simply let the pile set. Slowly it will become compost all by itself.

HOW DO YOU START A COMPOST BIN?

Some hardware stores sell compost bins. Or you can get a large wooden bin that measures about 30 inches (76 centimeters) wide by 30 inches deep by 30 inches high. Or just get some chicken wire to form a round "container" of about 30 inches in diameter and 35 inches (90 cm) in height. Then dump in your fallen leaves, grass clippings, and kitchen scraps. Mix them all together well. Slowly, they will form compost.

If you want to make compost more quickly, you need to turn the compost. Often two bins are used for turning compost. (There can also be a third bin for storing the compost that is ready to be spread on the garden.)

WHAT CAN GO INTO THE COMPOST?

Anything that comes from a plant or a tree can go into the compost. This type of "garbage" is called organic matter. If it's big like branches or vines or thick like orange peels, you should chop it into smaller pieces to help it start breaking down. An adult should supervise the chopping. Plus, animal manure from rabbits and chickens can be added to enrich the compost too. Don't put in meat scraps or dairy products. They attract animals.

CAN YOU MAKE COMPOST IF YOU DON'T HAVE A BACKYARD?

Some cities have composting programs. They collect yard waste and then compost it in big city piles. When it's composted, they let people take it to use in their gardens. Some schools have composting programs. They put leftovers from the cafeteria and leaves from the yard into the compost bin. Or they use a worm composting box indoors. Then they use the compost in a school garden.

WHAT MAKES THE GARBAGE TURN INTO COMPOST?

In the compost bin, tiny bacteria start breaking down the organic matter. Then fungi and protozoans join the bacteria in this breaking-down process. Later, centipedes, millipedes, beetles, and earthworms help too. This process of breaking down is called decay, or decomposition.

Try this simple experiment to see how composting works:
• Fill a large plant pot about one-third full of dirt.
• Chop up a few food scraps (an apple core, carrot scrapings, salad—no meat or dairy), and add them to the dirt in the pot.
• Add some more dirt to the pot.
• Turn the mixture with a spoon every few days, and keep it damp (not wet) by spraying or sprinkling with water. Always make sure that there is dirt on the top layer after you've turned the mixture over.
• Eventually the food scraps will "disappear." They've turned into compost. Now you can plant something in the compost and soil mixture.

WHY IS COMPOSTING IMPORTANT?
Much garbage thrown away each year is organic matter, which can be composted. The more we compost, the less garbage we'll have. Plus, compost is valuable. It puts important nutrients back into the soil. It makes the earth richer and helps plants grow. So composting helps the earth in many ways.

Text copyright © 2010 by Linda Glaser
Photographs copyright © 2010 by Shelley Rotner

All rights reserved. International copyright secured. No part of this book may be reproduced, stored in a retrieval system, or transmitted in any form or by any means—electronic, mechanical, photocopying, recording, or otherwise—without the prior written permission of Lerner Publishing Group, Inc., except for the inclusion of brief quotations in an acknowledged review.

Millbrook Press
A division of Lerner Publishing Group, Inc.
241 First Avenue North
Minneapolis, MN 55401 U.S.A.

Website address: www.lernerbooks.com

Library of Congress Cataloging-in-Publication Data

Glaser, Linda.
        Garbage helps our garden grow : a compost story / by Linda Glaser ;
    photographs by Shelley Rotner.
            p.   cm.
        ISBN: 978–0–7613–4911–2 (lib. bdg. : alk. paper)
        1. Compost—Juvenile literature. I. Rotner, Shelley. II. Title.
    S661.G584 2010
    635'.048975—dc22   2009023483

Manufactured in the United States of America
2 – DP – 2/1/11